C000271631

THIS BOOK BELONGS TO...

SOUTHAMPTON FC

Name:	Age:

Favourite player:

2021/2022

My Predictions...   **Actual...**

The Saints' final position:

The Saints' top scorer:

Premier League winners:

Premier League top scorer:

FA Cup winners:

EFL Cup winners:

Contributors: Peter Rogers

A TWOCAN PUBLICATION

©2021. Published by twocan under licence from Southampton Football Club.

Every effort has been made to ensure the accuracy of information within this publication but the publishers cannot be held responsible for any errors or omissions. Views expressed are those of the authors and do not necessarily represent those of the publishers or the football club. All rights reserved.

ISBN: 978-1-914588-03-7

PICTURE CREDITS: Action Images, Alamy, Press Association, Southampton Football Club.

PRINTED SEPTEMBER 2021

£9

CONTENTS

PREMIER LEAGUE
SQUAD
21/22

01 ALEX McCARTHY

POSITION:	Goalkeeper
DOB:	3 December 1999
COUNTRY:	England

Now in his fifth season with the Saints, goalkeeper Alex McCarthy arrived at St Mary's in August 2016 following a one-season spell at Crystal Palace.

Guilford-born McCarthy began his career with Reading and gained useful first-team experience with a host of loan moves before establishing himself firmly as the Royals' No1. He then joined Queens Park Rangers in 2014 before moving across London to Palace. McCarthy has now made over 100 league appearances for the Saints.

02 KYLE WALKER-PETERS

POSITION:	Defender
DOB:	13 April 1997
COUNTRY:	England

Former England U21 international Kyle Walker-Peters began his career with Tottenham Hotspur.

The 24-year-old defender progressed through the ranks at Tottenham and made a dozen Premier League appearances before joining Southampton on loan in the 2020 January transfer window. He made ten impressive appearances for the Saints while on loan during the Covid-19-interrupted campaign and the club made his move a permanent arrangement in August 2020.

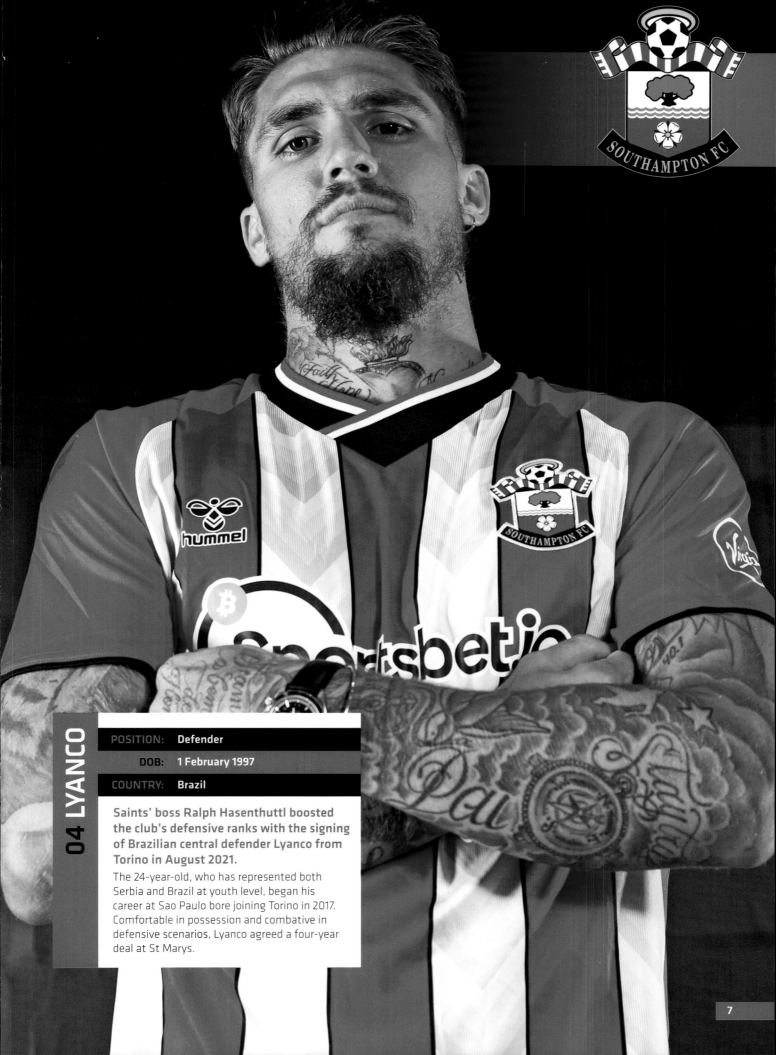

04 LYANCO

POSITION:	Defender
DOB:	1 February 1997
COUNTRY:	Brazil

Saints' boss Ralph Hasenthuttl boosted the club's defensive ranks with the signing of Brazilian central defender Lyanco from Torino in August 2021.

The 24-year-old, who has represented both Serbia and Brazil at youth level, began his career at Sao Paulo bore joining Torino in 2017. Comfortable in possession and combative in defensive scenarios, Lyanco agreed a four-year deal at St Marys.

CHE

Adams

10

The side-foot pass is one of the most accurate passing techniques over shorter distances. The ability to find one of your teammates with a pass, even when under severe pressure, and retain possession of the ball is an essential factor in the way the game is played today.

SOCCER SKILLS

EXERCISE ONE ▷▷▷▷

Set up a 10 x 10m grid. In one corner there are two players and on each of the other three corners there is one player.

Player A starts with the ball. Each player must pass the ball round the square in sequence then follow their pass. A passes to B then runs after his pass and takes up B's starting position. B passes to C and follows his pass to take C's position, and so on. All of the players must control the ball then pass it with the inside of their foot.

Key Factors

1. **Non-kicking foot alongside the ball.**
2. **Pass with the inside of the foot.**
3. **Strike through the middle of the ball.**
4. **Keep your eyes on the ball and your head steady.**

EXERCISE TWO ▷▷▷▷

The set up is the same as exercise one.

In this exercise the players pass the ball in sequence, A through to D, but do not follow their pass, remaining stationary.

As soon as A plays the first pass, E sets off racing around the outside of the starting point. The players must pass the ball as quickly and accurately as possible while under pressure from E, who cannot tackle but is effectively racing the ball round the square.

The same key factors apply in this exercise as in the first, but the players are required to be able to pass the ball accurately while under pressure.

Any team who can retain possession through good accurate passing will always make it very difficult for the opposition. The side-foot pass is one of the most accurate passing techniques.

PETER SHILTON ▷▷▷▷

England goalkeeper Peter Shilton joined Southampton from Nottingham Forest in 1982 and his move to The Dell saw him link up with former international teammates Kevin Keegan and Alan Ball.

Shilton was a star performer in the Saints' 1983/84 side which ended the season as First Division runners-up and FA Cup semi-finalists. He also represented England at the 1986 World Cup finals in Mexico where his displays helped the Three Lions reach the quarter-final stage.

Already a vastly experienced 'keeper when he arrived at Southampton, Shilton's presence gave real confidence to the defence playing in front of him as his signing proved a masterstroke by then Saints boss Lawrie McMenemy.

SAINTS HEROES

EYES

Always keeping a close eye on the ball, goalkeeper Shilton used his sight to judge the flight of crosses and the speed of shots heading his way. Sight is such a vital part of goalkeeping, particularly when quickly assessing whether to come for a ball or leave it for a defender.

VOICE

Charged with organising the defensive unit in front of him, goalkeeper Shilton would often be heard barking instructions to his teammates. With the whole pitch in his sight, it is an important part of the goalkeeper's role to advise teammates of the dangers he can spot.

HANDS

Blessed with the ability to quickly bring his hands into action to repel opposition's efforts on goal, Shilton could always be relied upon to pull off saves and use his hands effectively to either gather the ball or push it to safety.

FEET

Peter Shilton kept goal for Southampton long before the back-pass rule was introduced, however he still used his feet to great effect. His kicking could be relied upon to clear danger swiftly up-field and he would often sprint off his line to thwart attackers in a one-on-one situation.

```
A G F G O L D E N G O A L A A V C U R B
O C L E A N S H E E T N T X O A S A E V
D R I B B L I N G A Y H B L U C A T M I
E B P H R N R U T F F Y U R C V N S O F
A F F H I T T H E W O O D W O R K M J G
D I L C E N S X D T V R C G R G E O T S
B M A D J P Z E U I W J F N E A D E Z M
A R P K U L I E F S B M A M P I K O S R
L Q A T A T M S D O E M T R P J P Q P A
L Y V C P O A G O I D U A A I Y T N B I
S I W U E T G T A R N V B T K A H V W N
P R C L I N I C A L F I N I S H E R N B
E R Z N S T C H X M A M A M I E N L A O
C Q E H C N S H Y O S U J G L T U E M W
I O A F O S P T E W R O D B Z A M X T K
A J I N F F O X I N T H E B O X B F E I
L K A D E A N T Y V N R K B S Q I C G C
I M G F M U G I A N T K I L L I N G R K
S X P B U H E L G L O R T N O C L L A B
T H E B E A U T I F U L G A M E S P T T
```

SOCCER SEARCH

ALL OF THESE FOOTY TERMS ARE HIDDEN IN THE GRID, EXCEPT FOR ONE...
CAN YOU WORK OUT WHICH ONE?

Ball Control
Bicycle Kick
Boot it
Brace
Clean Sheet

Clinical Finisher
Cruyff Turn
Cup-tied
Dead-ball Specialist
Dribbling

Flip Flap
Fox in the Box
Gaffer
Giant-killing
Golden Goal

Hard Man
Hit the Woodwork
Magic Sponge
Man On
Nutmeg

Rainbow Kick
Skipper
Target Man
The Beautiful Game
Treble

PREMIER LEAGUE
SQUAD
21/22

05 JACK STEPHENS

POSITION:	Defender
DOB:	27 January 1994
COUNTRY:	England

Versatile defender Jack Stephens joined the Saints in April 2011 following a string of first-team outings for Plymouth Argyle.

With the ability to operate at right-back, central defence or at left-back, Stephens initially linked up with the Saints' U23 development squad before making his first-team debut in an FA Cup victory over Coventry City in January 2012. He has also taken in loan spells with Swindon Town, Middlesbrough and Coventry City before establishing himself at St Mary's with over a century of league appearances.

06 ORIOL ROMEU

POSITION:	Midfielder
DOB:	24 September 1991
COUNTRY:	Spain

A defensive ball-winning midfielder, Oriol Romeu joined the Saints from Premier League rivals Chelsea in the summer of 2015.

His presence in the team provides an important layer of protection in front of the back four and he is now one of the club's longest-serving players. An experienced and important member of the Saints squad, Romeu has amassed over 200 first-team appearances since arriving at St Mary's.

07 SHANE LONG

POSITION:	Forward
DOB:	22 January 1987
COUNTRY:	Republic of Ireland

An experienced Republic of Ireland international forward, Shane Long joined Southampton in August 2014 from Hull City.

Blessed with a great first touch and poacher's eye for goal - Long came to prominence with Reading before joining West Bromwich Albion and later the Tigers. He is another member of the current squad to have amassed over 200 games for the club.

08 JAMES WARD-PROWSE

POSITION:	Midfielder
DOB:	1 November 1994
COUNTRY:	England

A product of the Saints' famed youth Academy, midfielder James Ward-Prowse first joined the club at the age of eight.

A deep-lying midfield playmaker who is blessed with the ability to execute dead-ball situations with phenomenal accuracy, Ward-Prowse has progressed though the Academy system to make a first-team place his own. A full England international, Ward-Prowse was named Saints captain in 2020 and has now made over 300 appearances in a Southampton shirt.

SOUTHAMPTON FC

CLASSIC

FAN'TASTIC

Sammy Saint is hiding in the crowd in five places as fans celebrate Southampton bringing home the FA Cup in 1976. **Can you find him?**

DESIGN A KIT

Have a go at creating next season's home kit for the Saints!

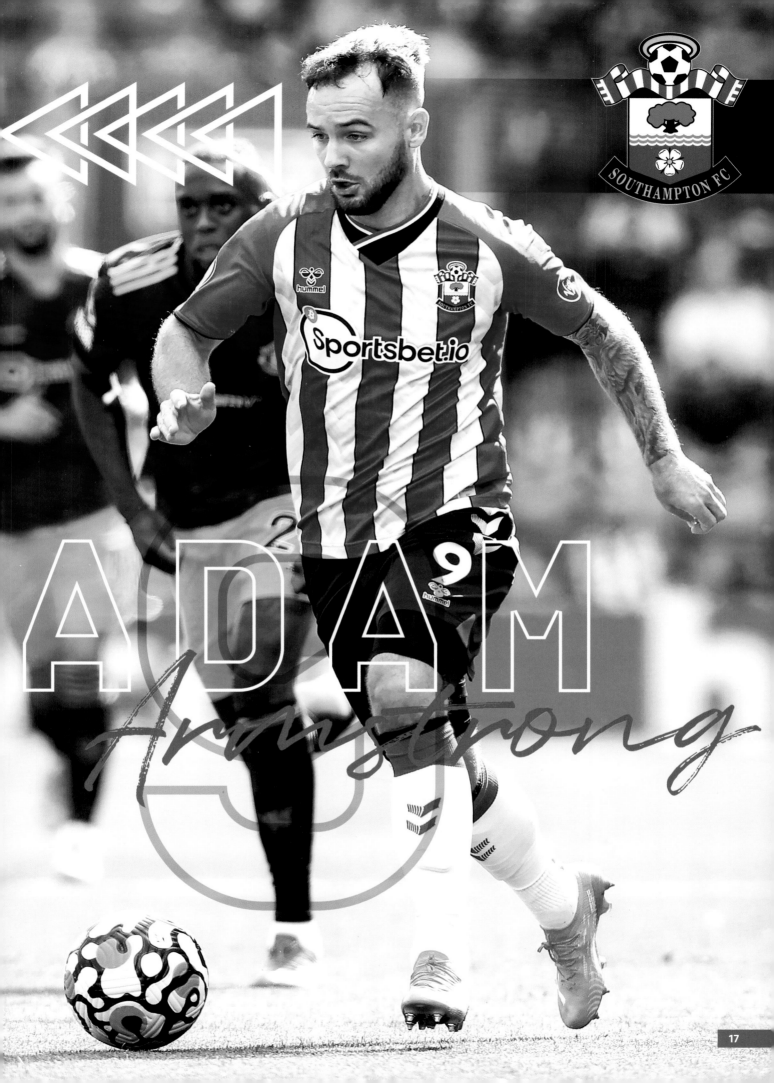

KITTED OUT

The Saints' red and white colours have been a proud and long-held tradition at the club. However, excitement and anticipation still surrounds the launch of every new Saints kit.

Each and every playing strip forms its own part of club history and supporters young and old will all have their own favourites. Let's take a look back at two of the best...

1995/96

Saints donned a classic look for their 1995/96 Premier League campaign with the second of four strips that were manufactured by Pony during the 1990s.

A traditional red and white striped shirt was enhanced with a trendy button collar and the club crest was housed on a red shield background and, together with the manufacturer's name and sponsor's branding, was placed on the chest area.

The black shorts had a red and black trim on the side panels with club crest and Pony branding on the front. The manufacturer's name also made an appearance on the front of the red and white banded socks.

DRESSED **TO IMPRESS**

A vital 3-1 victory over Manchester United in April 1996 proved the catalyst for the Saints' Premier League survival in 1995/96.

Dave Merrington's side ended the season in 17th place with 38 points and maintained their top-flight status on goal difference. Despite a struggle for league points, the club enjoyed an impressive FA Cup run that saw them reach the quarter-final stage.

HE WORE **IT WELL**

Club legend Matthew Le Tissier was once again a star performer in Saints 1995/96 great escape.

On target in the crucial 3-1 win over Manchester United at The Dell, Le Tissier also netted the only goal of the game to give Saints all three points away to Bolton Wanderers in their penultimate fixture.

In what was the club's historic final season at The Dell, the club continued with an in-house 'Saints' manufactured strip in 2000/01.

In a slight move away from conventional red and white stripes, the shirt was mainly white with a large red stripe in the centre and red panels under the arms - a theme that continued on the sleeves. The open-necked collar was black with a white trim and that design appeared on the cuffs too. The club crest, manufacturer's motif and sponsor's branding were housed on the chest area.

The all-black shorts had a red trim at the bottom and also carried the club crest and manufacturer's motif. The socks were black and topped with two red bands and had the word 'Saints' woven into the front.

DRESSED TO IMPRESS

Southampton signed off from life at The Dell in 2000/01 with a top-ten Premier League finish in what was a historic season in the club's rich history.

In an emotional final competitive game at the old ground, Saints edged a five-goal thriller with Arsenal and fittingly it was Matthew Le Tissier who scored the 89th-minute winner for what proved to be the club's final league goal at The Dell.

HE WORE IT WELL

Striker James Beattie topped the club's scoring charts in 2000/01 with a dozen goals, eleven of which came in the Premier League.

Beattie enjoyed a purple patch in November 2000 when he netted a brace at The Dell in a 3-2 victory over Chelsea and followed that up with another goal a week later in a 2-2 draw away to Sunderland. He was once again the Saints' man at the double when he made it back-to-back home braces as Aston Villa were beaten 2-0 on 18 November.

2000/01

PREMIER LEAGUE SQUAD 21/22

09 ADAM ARMSTRONG

POSITION:	Forward
DOB:	10 February 1997
COUNTRY:	England

Adam Armstrong wasted little time in introducing himself to the Saints faithful as he marked his Southampton debut with a goal against Everton on the opening day of the 2021/22 season.

An exciting summer signing from Blackburn Rovers, for whom he scored 28 goals at Championship level last season, 24-year-old Armstrong agreed a four-year deal at St Mary's in August 2021.

10 CHE ADAMS

POSITION:	Forward
DOB:	13 July 1996
COUNTRY:	Scotland

A mobile and robust forward, 25-year-old Che Adams was a summer 2019 signing from Birmingham City.

Patience was the key for Adams when he initially arrived at St Mary's and had to battle with Shane Long and Michael Obafemi to partner Danny Ings in attack. He ended his first season at the club with the Goal of the Season award for his 40-yard strike against Manchester City in July 2020. The Scotland international then netted nine Premier League goals last season before representing his country in the Euro 2020 finals.

SOUTHAMPTON FC

11 NATHAN REDMOND

POSITION:	Midfielder
DOB:	6 March 1995
COUNTRY:	England

Livewire midfielder Nathan Redmond is now entering his sixth season at St Mary's having joined the club from Norwich City in June 2016.

An exciting talent, whose tricky wing play and appetite to shoot for goal himself, often has fans up and off their seats. Redmond began his career with Birmingham City and has now played over 200 games for the Saints.

15 ROMAIN PERAUD

POSITION:	Defender
DOB:	22 September 1997
COUNTRY:	France

Capped by France at all youth levels from U17 to U21, left-back Romain Peraud joined Southampton in July 2021 from Ligue 1 club Brest.

Peraud began his career with Nice and took in a loan spell at Paris FC before joining Brest in 2019. He made his Saints' debut on the opening day of the 2021/22 campaign as Ralph Hasenhuttl's men travelled to Goodison Park.

Keeping fit and healthy is vital for all of us. So if you play footy for the school team or your local club, being fit and ready for action is sure to help you enjoy the game and perform to your very best.

For the players at Southampton, showing peak levels of fitness is essential if they want to feature in Ralph Hasenhuttl's team. Before anyone can think of pulling on the famous red and white shirt and taking to the pitch at St Mary's on a Saturday afternoon, they will have had to perform well in training at Staplewood and to have shown the manager, his coaches and fitness staff that they are fully fit and ready for the physical challenges that await them on a matchday.

Regardless of whether training takes place at the training ground or at the stadium, the players' fitness remains an all-important factor.

Of course, time spent working on training drills and playing small-sided games will help a player's fitness, but there is lots of work undertaken just to ensure maximum levels of fitness are reached. Away from the training pitches the professional players will spend a great deal of time in the gymnasium partaking in their own personal workouts. Bikes, treadmills and weights will all form part of helping the players reach and maintain a top level of fitness.

Over the course of a week the players will take part in many warm-up and aerobic sessions and even complete yoga and pilates classes to help with core strength and general fitness. The strength and conditioning coaches at the club work tirelessly to do all they can to make sure that the Southampton players you see in action on a matchday really are fighting fit for footy!

GET FIT for Footy

THEO
Walcott
32

It has been said that dribbling is a dying art. The pace of the modern game makes it more difficult, but there are players about, even in today's lightning fast conditions, who have the confidence to keep hold of the ball and take on defenders.

EXERCISE ONE ▷▷▷▷▷

As a warm-up exercise, players A and B each dribble a ball around a 20 x 10m grid, avoiding each other, but staying within the grid boundary lines.

They progress to a 'cat and mouse' race between the corners - the player with the most visits to each corner wins the race. One of the main problems in this exercise is avoiding the other player, and their ball.

EXERCISE TWO

Now for a more realistic exercise. Six players are used as shown, with three attackers and three defenders at any one time. When play starts, the players with the ball attack any of the three opposing goals, changing their target as they choose. The defenders have, simply, to stop their opposite number from scoring, but must not interfere with any other pair.

Key Factors

1. **Close control.**
2. **Quick change of direction.**
3. **Acceleration away from defender.**
4. **Feints, to wrong-foot defender.**
5. **Head up to see the whole picture.**

When the defenders win possession, they become the attackers, and go for goal themselves. This can be a very enjoyable practice, but also quite tiring.

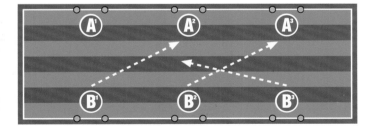

SOCCER
SKILLS

DRIBBLING ▷▷

SOUTHAMPTON FC

1 ANSWER

2 ANSWER

3 ANSWER

4 ANSWER

5 ANSWER

26

GUESS THE CLUB

Each football holds the clues to the identity of a Premier League or Football League club.

How quickly can you solve them?

6 ANSWER

7 ANSWER EST·1

8 ANSWER

9 ANSWER

10 ANSWER

ANSWERS ON PAGE 62

SQUAD
21/22

16 THIERRY SMALL

POSITION:	Defender
DOB:	1 August 2004
COUNTRY:	England

Born in Solihull, the left-back started his youth career at West Bromwich Albion before moving to Everton at 11-years-old.

Becoming a mainstay in Everton's under-23 side during the 2020/21 season, Small then became Everton's youngest-ever player when he made his first-team debut in January 2021. He was aged just 16 years and 176 days when he featured in the Toffees' FA Cup fourth round victory over Sheffield Wednesday.

17 STUART ARMSTRONG

POSITION:	Midfielder
DOB:	30 March 1992
COUNTRY:	Scotland

Inverness-born Stuart Armstrong began his professional career with Dundee United before joining Glasgow giants Celtic in 2015. After winning four Scottish Premier League titles, two Scottish Cups and two Scottish League Cups, the midfielder joined Saints in June 2018.

A regular face in the Southampton side following his arrival at St Mary's, the Scotland international has made over 100 appearances for the Saints and is in double figures for goals scored.

18 ARMANDO BROJA

POSITION:	Forward
DOB:	10 September 2001
COUNTRY:	Albania

Armando Broja joined Southampton in August 2021 when he agreed a season-long loan deal from Premier League rivals Chelsea.

Having progressed though the Blues' Academy set-up, he made his professional debut for Chelsea when he replaced Olivier Giroud in the final stages of a 4-0 victory over Everton in March 2020. Highly rated at Stamford Bridge, the Albanian international enjoyed a successful loan with Vitesse in 2020/21 and agreed a new five-year contract with his parent club prior to joining the Saints.

19 MOUSSA DJENEPO

POSITION:	Midfielder
DOB:	15 June 1998
COUNTRY:	Mali

Mali international Moussa Djenepo joined the Saints in June 2019 on a four-year deal from Belgian side Standard Liege.

The 23-year-old attacking midfielder netted his first goal for his new club in the 2-0 Premier League victory over Brighton in August 2019, while his second strike in Southampton colours secured a 1-0 win away to Sheffield United in September and was voted Goal of the Month. Ahead of the new 2021/22 campaign Djenepo had already amassed over 50 appearances for the Saints.

PLAYER OF THE SEASON

The official Southampton Football Club Player Awards for 2020/21 proved to be a cause for double celebration for Saints' captain...

JAMES WARD-PROWSE ▷▷▷▷▷

After fans voted the club skipper as the Virgin Media fans' Player of the Season, Ward-Prowse's teammates followed suit by confirming him as the Players' Player of the Season too.

Landing two such prestigious accolades capped off yet another great season at St Mary's for the popular midfielder who once again played every minute of the campaign for Ralph Hasenhuttl's side, contributing nine goals and seven assists.

He narrowly missed out on an incredible hat-trick of awards, coming close to picking up the club's Goal of the Season trophy too.

The Player of the Season awards were certainly a fitting recognition for Ward-Prowse in what was his first full season as Saints' skipper. The responsibility of wearing the armband and leading the team appeared to almost enhance his performances in a campaign that also saw him make a landmark 300th appearance for the club in January 2021.

Among his nine Premier League goals in 2020/21 was a first-half brace in the Saints' thrilling 4-3 victory away to Aston Villa in November 2020.

Ward-Prowse's fitness, stamina, consistency and reputation as a set-piece specialist continue to win him many admirers and at international level, he was named in England's provisional 33-man squad for the Euro 2020 finals. Sadly, he did not make the final squad, but that will do little to dampen his desire to add to the eight full England caps he had won as at the start of the 2021/22 campaign.

YOUNG PLAYER OF THE SEASON

The club's Young Player of the Season award was won by 22-year-old midfielder Nathan Tella. After making his first-team debut in Project Restart as the Saints cruised to a 3-0 victory away to Norwich City in June 2020, Tella enjoyed a breakthrough season at St Mary's in 2020/21.

In total, Tella featured in 22 first-team fixtures in all competitions last season and netted his first senior goal in the Saints' 3-1 victory over Fulham in May 2021.

A talented midfielder with a great future ahead of him, Tella will certainly be keen to add to his first-team experience in 2021/22.

NATHAN TELLA ▷▷▷▷

After scoring 59 goals in 155 games for Bristol Rovers, powerful striker Rickie Lambert joined Southampton in August 2009 for a fee in excess of £1M.

Lambert netted on his Saints debut and proved an instant success at St Mary's. He ended his first season as top scorer with 36 goals in all competitions and was also a Football League Trophy winner as Saints defeated Carlisle United at Wembley in March 2010.

Lambert's goals inspired the club to back-to-back promotion success in 2010/11 and 2011/12 as the Saints returned to the Premier League. He took the top flight by storm and his club form won him international recognition with England and a £4M move to Liverpool. In total, Lambert netted an impressive 117 goals for the Saints in 235 appearances for the club.

RICKIE LAMBERT ▷▷▷▷

SAINTS HEROES

ENCOURAGEMENT

As the focal point of the attack, Lambert could be relied upon to advise and encourage teammates to play the ball into areas where he could be most effective and cause danger to the opposition.

GOALS

Although a fair amount of Rickie's goals for Saints came from headers, he was pretty lethal with a trusty right foot too. An ace penalty taker he successfully converted all 34 of the spot-kicks he took in a Southampton shirt.

HEADERS

A good number of Rickie Lambert's Southampton goals came from headers. A real threat in the air, at 6ft 2ins Lambert had the power and height to out-jump defenders and then use his head to direct the ball past the 'keeper and into the net. Once the ball was in and around the six-yard box and in the air there was always a good chance Rickie would head it home.

CHEST CONTROL

As a strong centre-forward who led the Saints' attack so well, Rickie Lambert was blessed with a great ability to play with his back to goal and take the ball under control on his chest. He could then hold up play while others arrived in support or lay the ball off to a teammate.

TINO
Livramento
21

SOUTHAMPTON FC

33

Former St Mary's favourite Maya Yoshida is Southampton's most capped international player. Maya won 83 caps for Japan during his eight-year Saints career.

A consistent central defender, Yoshida joined the club from Dutch side VVV-Venlo in August 2012 and made his St Mary's bow in a 4-1 Premier League victory over Aston Villa and went on to form a solid partnership with Jose Fonte.

As a Southampton player, Yoshida featured in all three of Japan's group games in the 2014 World Cup finals in Brazil. After joining Italian club Sampdoria in 2020, he continued to play international football and made his 100th appearance for Japan in 2019. As at the end of the 2020/21 campaign he'd won 107 caps and scored eleven goals for his country.

MOST INTERNATIONAL CAPS ▷▷▷▷

RECORD
APPEARANCE
MAKER ▷▷▷▷

TOP ▷▷▷▷
GOALSCORER

Club legend Terry Paine proudly holds the record at the Saints' top appearance maker having played a colossal 815 times for the club between 1957 and 1974.

As an attack-minded player who predominantly operated on the right side of midfield, Paine was a vital member of the 1959/60 side which won promotion as Division Three champions. A supremely confident player, Paine was blessed with great ability to cross a ball with devastating accuracy, a skill which forwards such as Ron Davies and Martin Chivers thrived upon.

Named Southampton captain in 1961, Terry won the first of his 19 England caps in 1963. Awarded an MBE for his services to football when he retired, Paine also has one of the hospitality suites at St Mary's Stadium named after him.

Ace marksman Mick Channon holds the record as Southampton Football Club's top goalscorer. In two separate spells with the club, 1965 to 1977 and 1979 to 1982, Mick made a total of 602 appearances for the Saints and found the back of the opposition's net on 228 occasions.

He began his long and successful playing career at The Dell and marked his league debut with a goal as a fresh faced 17-year-old against Bristol City in April 1966.

His impressive goals-to-games ratio saw him win 46 caps for England and net 21 goals at international level. A member of the Saints' 1976 FA Cup winning side, he joined Manchester City in the summer of 1977 but after failing to settle in the north west, he returned to his spiritual home of The Dell in September 1979.

RECORD MAKERS

A SELECTION OF PLAYERS, GAMES, FACTS & FIGURES WHICH ALL SHAPE THE CLUB'S PROUD HISTORY...

RECORD ATTENDANCE ▷▷▷▷

As we all know there are few better places to be than inside a packed St Mary's Stadium and cheering the Saints on to victory. The current capacity at today's modern all-seater St Mary's is 32,384 with the record attendance for a Saints' fixture being set when 32,363 fans witnessed a 4-0 final-day victory over Coventry City on 28 April 2012 as the team sealed promotion to the Premier League.

Prior to moving to St Mary's in 2001, the club's previous home was The Dell where a record crowd of 31,044 were shoehorned in to watch a First Division match with Manchester United on 8 October 1969.

Forward Theo Walcott progressed though the Saints' Academy to become the youngest-ever player to appear in the club's first team.

The teenager made history when he replaced striker Kenwyne Jones in the 73rd minute of Southampton's goalless Championship meeting with Wolverhampton Wanderers at St Mary's on Saturday, 6 August 2005. Walcott was aged just 16 years 143 days old when he made his debut and his appearance saw him supersede Danny Wallace the club's youngest player.

Walcott later went on to enjoy international stardom with England as a top quality Premier League performer with Arsenal and Everton. After a successful loan spell back at St Mary's during the 2020/21 campaign, Walcott agreed a permanent two-year deal with the Saints in the summer of 2021 following the conclusion of his contract at Goodison Park.

YOUNGEST PLAYER ▷▷▷▷

PREMIER LEAGUE
SQUAD
21/22

20 WILL SMALLBONE

POSITION:	Midfielder
DOB:	21 February 2000
COUNTRY:	Republic of Ireland

Will Smallbone progressed through the club's Academy system to earn a first professional contract with Southampton in February 2017.

He enjoyed a fairytale first-team debut as he opened the scoring in the Saints' 2-0 FA Cup third round triumph over Huddersfield Town in January 2020. A first taste of Premier League action came the next month in Saints' 2-0 victory over Aston Villa. After really starting to make his mark on the first-team scene, Smallbone suffered an anterior cruciate ligament injury in January 2021 in a match away to Leicester City. The injury will delay his involvement at the start of the 2021/22 campaign.

21 TINO LIVRAMENTO

POSITION:	Defender
DOB:	12 November 2002
COUNTRY:	England

Just like Saints' teammate Armando Broja, Tino Livramento is a product of the Chelsea youth Academy. The teenage right-back was voted the Blues' Academy Player of the Season in 2020/21 and was named on the bench for Premier League fixtures.

Feeling his opportunities of first-team football would be better served at St Mary's, the England U19 international put pen to paper on a move to Southampton in August 2021. He made his Premier League debut in the Saints' opening game of the season away to Everton.

SOUTHAMPTON FC

22 MOHAMMED SALISU

POSITION:	Defender
DOB:	17 April 1999
COUNTRY:	Ghana

Ghanaian central defender Mohammed Salisu progressed through the ranks at Spanish club Real Valladolid before moving to the Premier League when the Saints triggered a buy-out clause in his Valladolid contract in the summer of 2020.

The powerfully built 6ft 3in defender agreed a four-year deal at St Mary's and debuted in the February 2021 FA Cup victory over Wolverhampton Wanderers. He then went on to feature in a dozen Premier League fixtures at the end of the 2020/21 campaign.

23 NATHAN TELLA

POSITION:	Midfielder
DOB:	5 July 1999
COUNTRY:	England

Midfielder Nathan Tella capped off an excellent 2020/21 season at St Mary's by landing the club's Young Player of the Season award.

After making his first-team debut in Project Restart as the Saints cruised to a 3-0 victory away to Norwich City in June 2020, Tella featured in 22 first-team fixtures in all competitions last season and netted his first senior goal in the Saints' 3-1 victory over Fulham in May 2021.

IMPOSSIBLE FOOTY Decisions

WOULD YOU RATHER...

Have to play the rest of your football games in 35 degree heat or a blizzard?

WOULD YOU RATHER...

Have Adam Armstrong's ability to score goals or Alex McCarthy's ability to save them?

WOULD YOU RATHER...

Have a pause button or a rewind button for your life?

WOULD YOU RATHER...

Have unlimited battery life on all your devices or free wifi wherever you go?

WOULD YOU RATHER...

Run 100 laps of the pitch or complete 200 burpees?

WOULD YOU RATHER...

Score the FA Cup final winning goal against your rivals in your only game for Southampton or play 300 games for the Saints in League One?

WOULD YOU RATHER...

Be remembered for a terrible footy howler or be forgotten completely?

WOULD YOU RATHER...

Sell your best player to your biggest rivals for £50m or sell him abroad for £20m?

WOULD YOU RATHER...

Have to take a penalty against Alex McCarthy or have James Ward-Prowse take a penalty against you?

WOULD YOU RATHER...

Sit right at the back during a game or have the best seats in the stadium, but not be allowed to eat, drink or use the bathroom?

Be the star in League Two Or a squad player in the Premier League?

WOULD YOU RATHER...

Southampton win the FA Cup or England win the World Cup?

WOULD YOU RATHER...

Your match superstition be wearing the same socks for a season or the same underwear for a month?

WOULD YOU RATHER....

Lose on television or win with nobody watching?

WOULD YOU RATHER...

Have a long, average playing career or have a short, fantastic career cut short by injury?

WOULD YOU RATHER...

Lose to your arch-rivals twice and finish top or beat them twice and finish bottom?

WOULD YOU RATHER...

Clean the dressing room toilet with your toothbrush or the floor with your tongue?

Play only five minutes for Southampton or win the Premier League

WOULD YOU RATHER...

Have to wear every shirt inside out or every pair of pants backwards?

WOULD YOU RATHER...

Give up your mobile phone for a month or bathing for a month?

WOULD YOU RATHER...

Be alone all your life or surrounded by rival supporters?

WOULD YOU RATHER...

Play for Southampton and always lose Or sit on the bench and the Saints and always win?

WOULD YOU RATHER...

The half-time menu got rid of pies or pop?

WOULD YOU RATHER...

Become a legendary manager

WAYNE BRIDGE ▷▷▷▷

Southampton-born left-back Wayne Bridge joined the club as a trainee back in 1996 and turned professional two years later.

One of a small group of players to have played for the club at both The Dell and St Mary's - Bridge was voted the club's Player of the Season in 2000/01 in what was the team's final campaign at their old ground.

A consistent performer with high levels of fitness, Bridge made 113 consecutive Premier League appearances for the Saints in a career which saw him play 173 times for the club. His outstanding club form saw him win his first of 36 international caps for England in February 2002. He moved on to Chelsea in the summer of 2003 and became a Premier League winner while at Stamford Bridge in 2004/05.

SAINTS HEROES

TEMPERAMENT

Often faced with containing dangerous wingers, Wayne Bridge had the perfect mindset for defending. He very rarely lost concentration and always kept his cool. In the heat of any on-field duel, Bridge kept his mind on the task in hand and more often than not came out on top in one-on-one situations.

PASSING SKILLS

Always comfortable with the ball at his feet, Bridge was an accomplished ball-playing defender who could always be relied upon to bring the ball out of defence and help the side turn defence into attack.

RALLYING CALL

One of the first names on the teamsheet throughout his time at Southampton, Bridge's consistency and reliability soon won him the respect of his teammates. His ability to lead and inspire those around him was there for all to see. Always there with an encouraging call to teammates, Wayne led by example, but was never afraid to let players know if standards had dropped.

QUICK ON HIS HEELS

Wayne Bridge was always alive and alert to danger and when it occurred he was quick on his heels to track back and tackle opponents. Not only was he swift over the ground, but he was also quick to leap and win headed duels too.

MOHAMMED
Salisu

ALL KITTED OUT

The Saints' red and white colours have been a proud and long-held tradition at the club. However, excitement and anticipation still surrounds the launch of every new Saints kit.

Each and every playing strip forms its own part of club history and supporters young and old will all have their own favourites. Let's take a look back at another two of the best...

In 2010/11 the Saints and kit manufacturer Umbro marked the club's 125-year anniversary in style as they produced an unsponsored playing strip to replicate what was worn at the time of Southampton's formation back in 1885.

An all-white shirt with a thick red sash had an open-necked white collar with the club crest sitting proudly on the chest and the manufacturer's motif housed tastefully in white on the red sash.

The all-white shorts had a thin neat red trim at the bottom with the club crest and Umbro logo on the front. The socks were a solid black offering with the Umbro logo woven into the fabric and situated on the shin pad area.

2010/11

DRESSED **TO IMPRESS**

Under the management of Alan Pardew, Southampton ended a two-season spell in League One with promotion back to the Championship in what was the perfect ending to the club's 125th year.

Despite a slow start to the season, Saints soon found a winning formula and ended the campaign as runners-up to Brighton. Season highlights included a 6-0 hammering of Oldham Athletic before over 31,000 fans packed into St Mary's to celebrate promotion on the final day of the season.

HE WORE **IT WELL**

For a second successive season, striker Rickie Lambert was once again the Saints' leading marksman in 2010/11.

Lambert again topped the 20-goal mark and all of his 21 goals came in the promotion-winning League One campaign. The former Bristol Rovers man formed an impressive partnership with Lee Barnard who himself netted 14 league goals.

The Saints' 2012/13 strip saw kit manufacturer Umbro make a major change to the appearance of the Southampton team with a home shirt that was predominantly red with a thin white pinstripe.

On appearance the shirt looked almost a solid red but did have thin white pinstripes on the chest area while the red v-neck collar had a small white trim. The club crest, manufacturer's logo and sponsor's branding were all housed on the traditional chest area.

The all-red shorts carried the club crest and Umbro motif on the legs, while the red socks had four white bands and the manufacturer's logo displayed on the front.

DRESSED TO IMPRESS

The 2012/13 campaign saw a mid-season change of manager at St Mary's as Mauricio Pochettino replaced Nigel Adkins in the Saints hot-seat.

Back in the Premier League after a seven-year absence, the Saints maintained their top-flight status with a 14th-placed finish some five points clear of the relegation zone. After four straight defeats at the beginning of the campaign, Saints registered their first league win of the season when they defeated Aston Villa 4-1 at St Mary's. Season highlights also included home victories over Liverpool and Chelsea.

HE WORE IT WELL

The form of defensive midfielder Morgan Schneiderlin played a vital part in Southampton's 2012/13 season.

Playing at Premier League level for the first time in his career, Schneiderlin played in 36 of the Saints' 38-game league programme and also netted five goals - including the opening strike in the 3-1 home win over Liverpool in March 2013.

2012/13

24 MOHAMED ELYOUNOUSSI

POSITION:	Forward
DOB:	4 August 1994
COUNTRY:	Norway

A summer 2018 signing from Basel, Norwegian international forward Mohamed Elyounoussi agreed a five-year deal at St Mary's and debuted in the Saints' opening game of the 2018/19 campaign against Burnley.

With the ability to play on either wing or through the middle, the 27-year-old made 17 appearances in all competitions in his first season with the Saints. Unable to replicate the impressive scoring rate he displayed in France, Elyounoussi spent both the 2019/20 and 2020/21 campaigns on loan with Celtic.

27 IBRAHIMA DIALLO

POSITION:	Midfielder
DOB:	8 March 1999
COUNTRY:	France

A real box-to-box midfielder, Ibrahima Diallo joined Southampton from Ligue 1 side Brest in October 2020.

Capped by France at U21 level, Diallo made his Saints debut in the thrilling 3-3 Premier League draw with Chelsea at Stamford Bridge on 17 October 2020. Across 22 Premier League outings in 2020/21, Diallo displayed both a solid range of passing skills and a real desire to win the ball whenever out of possession.

SOUTHAMPTON FC

32 THEO WALCOTT

POSITION:	Midfielder
DOB:	16 March 1989
COUNTRY:	England

A player who needs little introduction to Saints fans, Theo Walcott burst onto the scene at St Mary's back in 2005 as the club's youngest player at 16 years 143 days old when he appeared in a Championship fixture against Wolverhampton Wanderers.

A high-profile move to the Premier League with Arsenal followed for Walcott who has also scored eight goals in 47 games for England and played for Everton. He returned to St Mary's as a full-time Saints player in May 2021 having spent the previous season on loan from Everton.

35 JAN BEDNAREK

POSITION:	Defender
DOB:	16 March 1989
COUNTRY:	Poland

Polish international defender Jan Bednarek was another member of the Saints' squad to feature in the Euro 2020 finals, with the 25-year-old playing in all three of his country's group games.

After joining the Saints from Lech Poznan in July 2017, Bednarek debuted in a League Cup tie with Wolves at St Mary's and has since made a century of Premier League appearances for the club.

SOUTHAMPTON FC

Sportsbet.io

JAMES
Ward-Prowse

One of a player's greatest assets is the ability to win the ball. The following exercise can be used to improve a player's tackling abilities.

EXERCISE ▷▷▷▷▷

Set up a 10m x 20m grid.

In this two-on-two exercise, the aim of the game is to score a goal by taking the ball past the two opposing defenders, to the end line, and stand on the ball. The defenders just have to stop them.

As well as producing plenty of opportunities for the defenders to tackle, this session will test the defenders' abilities to work together, and communicate.

Key Factors

1. **Be patient - do not dive in.**
2. **Stay on your feet if possible.**
3. **Time the tackle with bodyweight behind it.**
4. **Be determined to win it.**

The reason that great players win so many tackles is not just because they know how to tackle and have good technique, it is because they have big hearts and are determined to win their challenges on the pitch.

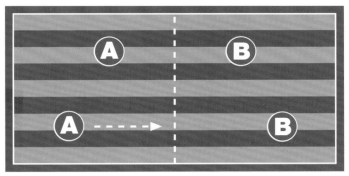

SOCCER SKILLS

TACKLING ▷▷

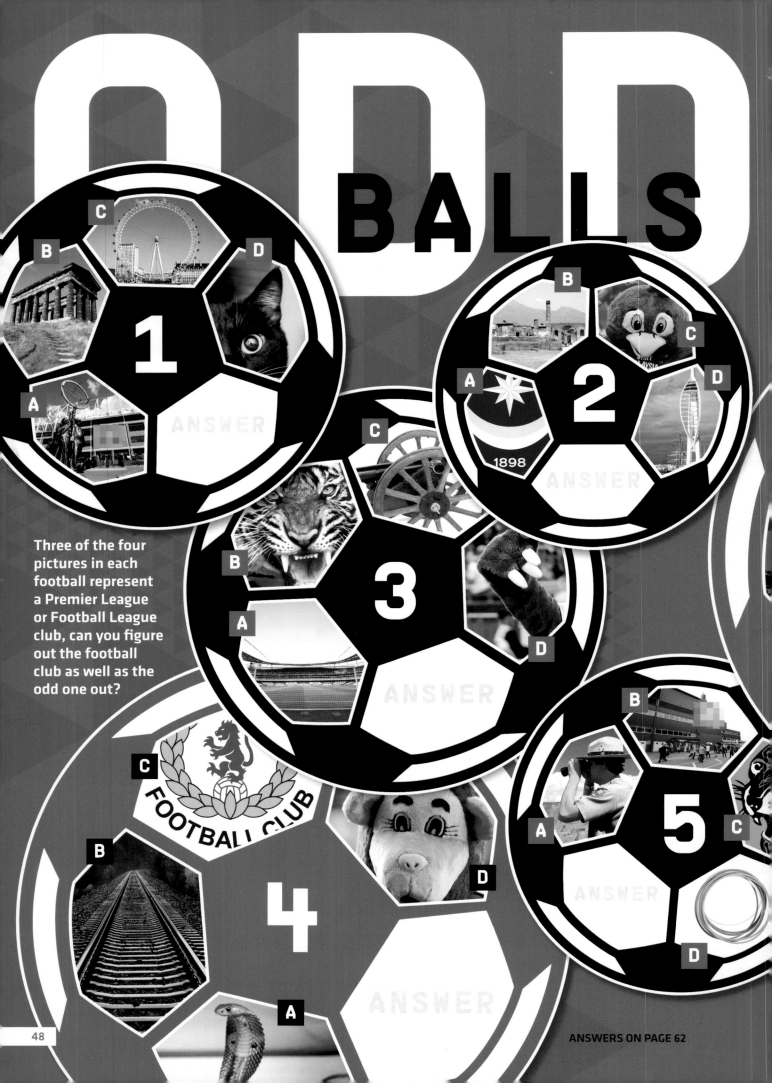

ODD BALLS

Three of the four pictures in each football represent a Premier League or Football League club, can you figure out the football club as well as the odd one out?

ANSWERS ON PAGE 62

SOUTHAMPTON FC

6

7

8

9

10

49

GOAL
of the Season

DANNY INGS ▶▶▶▶
V LIVERPOOL · JANUARY 2021

SOUTHAMPTON FC

JAMES WARD-PROWSE ▶▶▶▶
V NEWCASTLE · FEBRUARY 2021

CHE ADAMS ▶▶▶▶
V SHEFFIELD UNITED · MARCH 2021

Skipper James Ward-Prowse had a highly successful time at the Saints' 2020/21 Player Awards, but he was denied a hat-trick of titles by teammate Danny Ings who pipped him to the club's Goal of the Season trophy.

Ward-Prowse was hopeful his stunning free-kick against Newcastle United in February would see him add the Goal of the Season to his Player of the Season and Players' Player of the Season accolades.

Another effort in the running for the Goal of the Season award was Che Adams' strike in the Saints' 2-0 Premier League victory at Sheffield United in March. However, it was Ings' sensational lobbed effort that gave Southampton a 1-0 home win over Liverpool that won the day.

Ings' quick thinking saw him open the scoring against his former club after just two minutes with his seventh Premier League goal of the campaign and saw the Saints get the calendar year of 2021 off to a winning start. Ings' beautifully weighted lob over Liverpool goalkeeper Alisson was the 50th Premier League goal of his career - 36 of which came in a Southampton shirt.

Ings ended the season as the club's leading scorer with 13 goals, a dozen of which came in the Premier League. He was also on target at international level in 2020/21, netting England's third and final goal in a 3-0 friendly victory over Wales at Wembley in October 2020. His overhead kick against the Welsh was his first goal at international level, but despite his exceptional club form throughout 2020/21, he was overlooked for England's Euro 2020 squad.

TRUE
COLOURS

Have fun
colouring in
this picture of
Saints Star
Oriol Romeu

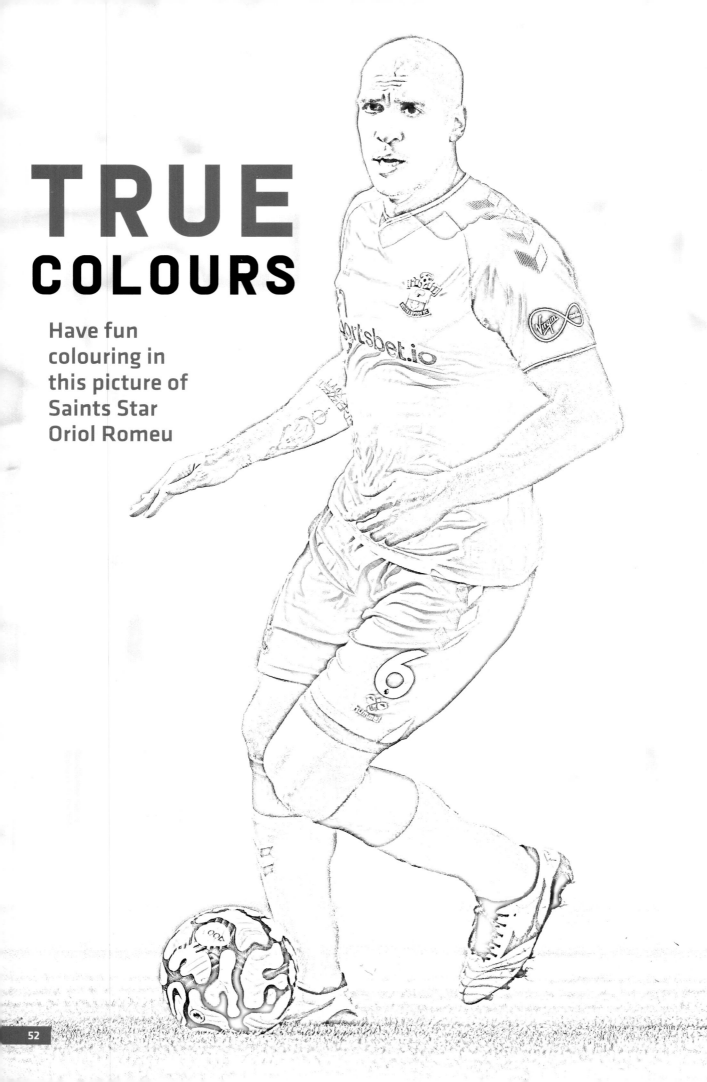

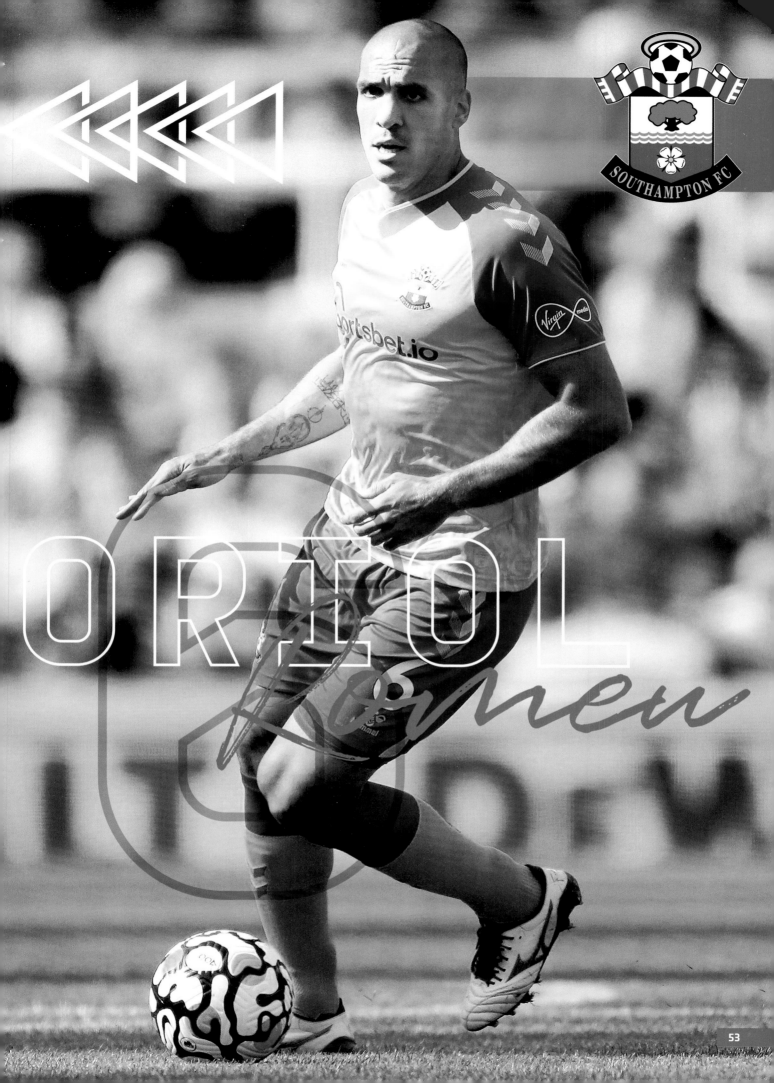

ORIOL Romeu

SQUAD 21/22

41 HARRY LEWIS

POSITION:	Goalkeeper
DOB:	17 March 1988
COUNTRY:	England

Young goalkeeper Harry Lewis is another graduate from the Saints' Academy set-up and now forms part of the club's first team goalkeeping options.

His first-team debut came in the 2017 FA Cup third round tie away to Norwich City. After playing in the 2-2 draw with the Canaries, Lewis then kept his maiden clean sheet at first-team level in the St Mary's replay. The following season saw him gain valuable experience when he made 39 appearances in all competitions during a season-long loan with Dundee United.

43 YAN VALERY

POSITION:	Defender
DOB:	22 February 1999
COUNTRY:	France

Young French defender Jan Valery made the brave move to depart his homeland and join the Saints' Academy in 2015.

After impressing with a series of quality performances at youth level he was handed a first-team debut in a League Cup tie away to Leicester City in November 2018. The speedy full-back grabbed that opportunity with both hands and followed it up with a Premier League debut against Manchester United just four days later. As at the end of the 2020/21 campaign he had made 40 first-team appearances for the Saints and taken in a loan spell in the Championship with Birmingham City.

44 FRASER FORSTER

POSITION:	Goalkeeper
DOB:	17 March 1988
COUNTRY:	England

England international goalkeeper Fraser Forster joined the Saints from Celtic ahead of the 2014/15 season.

The giant 6ft 7in stopper began his career with Newcastle United and enjoyed an impressive loan spell at Norwich City where he helped the Canaries win the League One title in 2009/10. Two successful loan spells with Celtic then resulted in a permanent switch to Parkhead. Firmly the first choice 'keeper at St Mary's following his transfer south of the border, Forster has had to battle with Alex McCarthy and Angus Gunn for first-team opportunities in recent seasons.

SOUTHAMPTON FC

Can you identify these six former Saints from the clues given? Good luck!

1. WHO AM I?

I was born in Newcastle in 1970

I began my career as an apprentice at Southampton

I marked my full debut for the Saints with a hat-trick

I scored 30 goals in 63 international appearances for England

I'm currently a regular pundit on Match of the Day

3. WHO AM I?

I began my career with my hometown club

I joined Southampton in the summer of 2012

I scored my first Premier League goal for the Saints against Spurs

I won my one and only England cap as a Southampton player

I left St Mary's to join a Premier League rival in the summer of 2017

GUESS WHO

2. WHO AM I?

I was the last line of defence throughout my career

I joined the Saints from Sunderland in the summer of 2006

Southampton were the seventh and final club of my career

I was part of a Saints' squad that won back-to-back promotions in 2010/11 and 2011/12

My long career at St Mary's was rewarded with a testimonial match in May 2016

4. WHO AM I?

I was born in Johannesburg in 1986

In the early part of my Saints' career I took in loan spells at Walsall and AFC Bournemouth

George Burley handed me my first start in a Southampton shirt

In 2007 I netted a hat-trick for the club in a 5-2 victory over Barnsley

I left the Saints in July 2009 to join a Premier League side

5. WHO AM I?

I was born in Southampton in 1980

I began my career at the Saints Academy

I played for seven other league clubs later in my career

I made more appearances for Southampton than any of my other clubs

I won 36 caps for England

6. WHO AM I?

I first sampled English football with a loan move to Crystal Palace

I joined Southampton in the 2010 January transfer window

I was voted Saints' Player of the Year in the 2010/11 season

In 2014 I was appointed as the club's captain

I made 260 league appearances for the Saints between 2010 and 2017

ANSWERS ON PAGE 62

The most popular Southampton player of the modern era, midfield magician Matthew Le Tissier scored 209 goals for the club in 540 outings between 1986 and 2002.

A technically-gifted midfielder, Le Tissier had a wonderful eye for goal and amazing vision which enabled him to create chances for teammates. Blessed with excellent control, technique, balance and dribbling skills, Le Tissier was simply a joy to watch and a loyal one-club servant.

A constant threat from set-play situations, Le Tissier had an outstanding success rate at penalties - converting 47 out of 48 spot kicks he took for the Saints. One of the very best Premier League players of all time - Le Tissier was also capped by England on eight occasions.

MATTHEW LE TISSIER ▷▷▷▷

SAINTS HEROES

INTELLIGENCE

A player's football intelligence is often spoken about and Matthew had it in abundance. He had the skill of making time on the ball, orchestrating the pattern of play and playing creative forward balls. He also had that ability of knowing the runs a teammate would make and the skill to find them with the minimum of fuss.

EYE FOR AN OPENING

Not only was Matthew extremely comfortable on the ball but he also showed great vision and awareness on the pitch. He appeared to have the perfect eye for a quick defence-splitting pass to help the Saints mount another attack.

QUICK FEET

Naturally blessed with exceptional close control, Matthew Le Tissier had the ability to unlock even the tightest of defences. Always indentified as the team's playmaker, Le Tissier proved to be a tricky player for opposition to get to grips with.

ADVICE

In his latter years at the club, Le Tissier used his experience and knowledge gained from playing at the top level for club and country to help the younger players in the Southampton team.

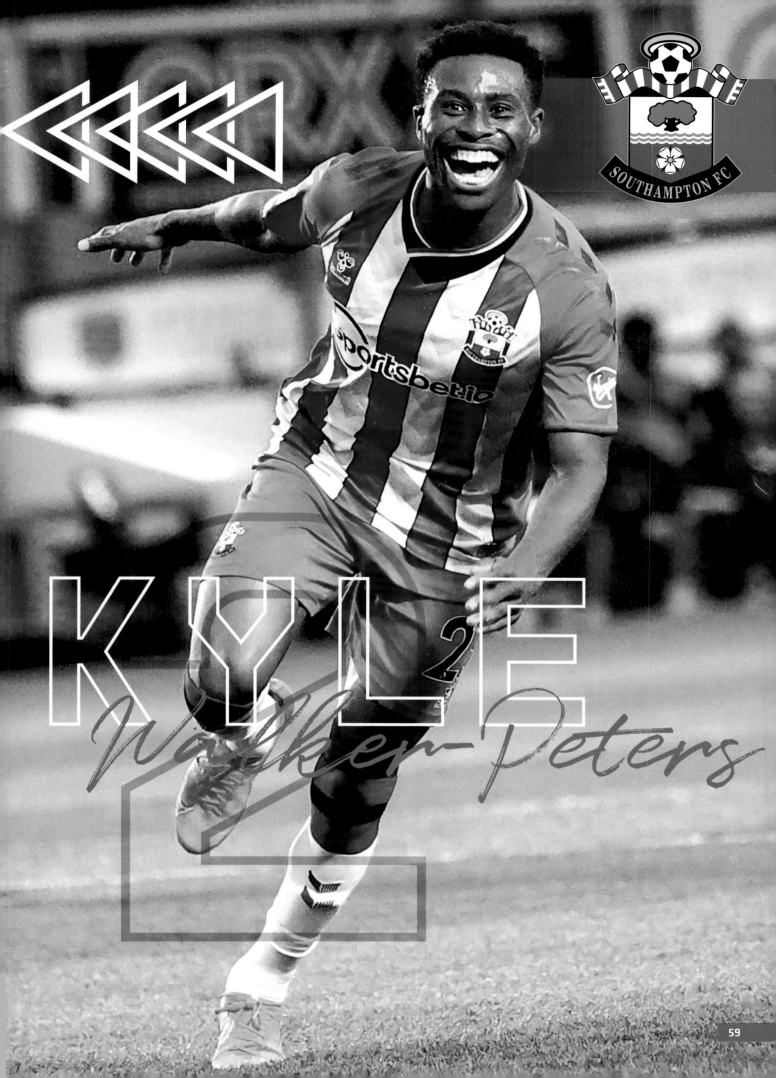

KYLE
Walker-Peters

FAST >> FORWARD

Do your predictions for 2021/22 match our own?

PREMIER LEAGUE TOP SCORER

Anthony Martial

PREMIER LEAGUE WINNERS

Manchester United

PREMIER LEAGUE RUNNERS-UP

Chelsea

FA CUP WINNERS
Southampton

FA CUP RUNNERS-UP
Leeds United

LEAGUE CUP WINNERS
Arsenal

LEAGUE CUP RUNNERS-UP
Leicester City

CHAMPIONSHIP WINNERS
Fulham

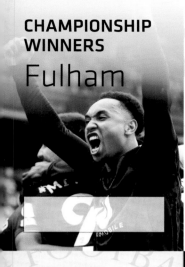

CHAMPIONSHIP RUNNERS-UP
Derby County

CHAMPIONSHIP PLAY-OFF WINNERS
Reading

CHAMPIONSHIP TOP SCORER
Ivan Cavaleiro

SAINTS TOP SCORER
Adam Armstrong

SAINTS PLAYER OF THE YEAR
James Ward-Prowse

CHAMPIONS LEAGUE WINNERS
Barcelona

CHAMPIONS LEAGUE RUNNERS-UP
Real Madrid

EUROPA LEAGUE WINNERS
West Ham United

EUROPA LEAGUE RUNNERS-UP
Lazio

ANSWERS

PAGE 11
SOCCER SEARCH

Bicycle Kick.

PAGE 14
CLASSIC FAN'TASTIC

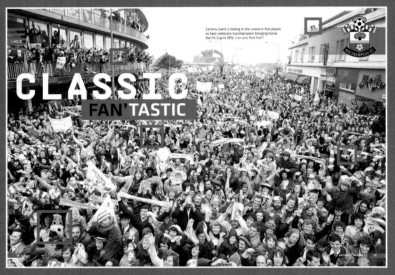

PAGE 26
GUESS THE CLUB

1. Newcastle United. 2. Wigan Athletic. 3. Leeds United.
4. Charlton Athletic. 5. Coventry City. 6. AFC Wimbledon.
7. Liverpool. 8. Millwall. 9.Wolverhampton Wanderers.
10. Nottingham Forest.

PAGE 48
ODD BALLS

1. Sunderland, C. 2. Portsmouth, C. 3. Arsenal, B.
4. Crewe Alexandra, A. 5. Queens Park Rangers, C.
6. Crystal Palace, B. 7. Tottenham Hotspur, B.
8. Reading, B. 9. Birmingham City, C.
10. West Ham United, D.

PAGE 56
GUESS WHO?

1. Alan Shearer. 2. Kelvin Davis. 3. Jay Rodriguez.
4. Andrew Surman. 5. Wayne Bridge. 6. Jose Fonte.